Things Nobody Tells You When You're Growing Up

by

Fiona Clark

For all those who share in the journey.

For D and O, for being their own wonderful selves, and for their treasured love.

And for D, for his never-ending love, support, patience and encouragement.

Things Nobody Tells You When You're Growing Up

by

Fiona Clark

ISBN: 9798607709723

Cover design by: Art Painter
Library of Congress Control Number: 2018675309
Printed in the United States of America

Table of Contents

About the Author

Fiona Clark is a writer, teacher, speaker and researcher, living and working in the UK. She studied *Teaching Emotional Resilience to Children and Adolescents* at the University of Pennsylvania. She is also a University of Nottingham alumnus, and a member of the National Association of Writers in Education.

A teacher and leader in schools for over two decades, Fiona now regularly takes up the role of writer in residence at schools across the UK, running creative writing workshops for school children. Evidence gathered through a Knowledge Exchange programme with University College London, shows that Fiona's workshops improve children's writing skills, improve well-being, boost self-esteem and increase confidence.

Fiona is a proud mum of girls, a wife, an amateur pianist and a keen jogger.

What is this book all about?

This book might be called a 'self-help' book. By design, the purpose of this book is to help you to help yourself. Growing up can feel like such a private matter as each individual has individual experiences. One thing links us all however is that as we grow, we start to feel self-doubt about some things - not being 100% sure about things and feeling like we're a bit lost as to what to do at times. This self-doubt can mean we feel unsure and reluctant to ask others about our thoughts and feelings. After all, we don't want to run the risk of anyone laughing at what might be a perfectly normal question. Sometimes people laugh out of embarrassment if we ask a question. They might not know what to say and it might trigger a response from them that leaves us feeling humiliated. So, a self-help book can enable you to start to address things in a private way.

After reading this book, or as you read it, you might feel like talking to a trusted grown-up, like a teacher or a relative, about certain parts of it. It might give you the confidence to talk openly about your experiences and maybe even feel a bit better about things that might be causing you any problems. Talking to the right person can help with a lot of things in life and that applies to us all, grown-ups and children.

In particular, the intention of this book is to share with you some things about life. It might also help you to explore all the types of things that might be going on with you and will hopefully help you to steer your way safely through the sometimes-rocky waters of life.

Not only will this book tell you things that nobody tells you when you're growing up; it's also about what kind of things that might be going on inside your head as you grow up. Lots of conversations and thoughts go on in people's heads as they talk to themselves and tell themselves different stuff at different times of the day. We call this internal chatter. It's a bit like having a radio on inside your head.

What we also want to do is to try to promote the good stuff you're telling yourself, while hopefully quieten the not so good stuff. So, let's get started. No time to lose.

You might be reading this book sitting in a room in a school, or you might be at home in your bedroom, or a bookstore or a library. Wherever you are, remember, you can dip in and out of this book at any time. It's designed that way with short sections that don't take too long to read. You can also re-read sections at times when you feel it is helpful. People often re-read self-help books after they've read them the first time, whenever the occasion arises.

This book is designed as a springboard to help you to open your mind to living your life in ways that are positive. It aims to promote positive mental health and well-being.

And remember, no matter what your age, it is best to talk to a doctor or medical professional if you need expert help with your physical or mental health.

Let's Get Started!

Let's get going.

Hi. If you've picked up this book because you are interested in finding out more about the mystery of growing up, then you've come to the right place. And wowsers, growing up can be tough sometimes. There are times when it can make you feel like you're being pulled in all directions and you can wind up in a knot. One word often used to describe growing up is 'confusing'. Your feelings can be confusing and the things happening around you can be crazy at times. Quite often children are left wondering two questions during each situation they face:

What on earth is going on in my life right now?

and

Is what I'm feeling 'normal'?

Growing up is different for everyone. What **you** experience is normal for you. Don't let anyone tell you that you're odd or strange because whatever you are feeling, it is your truth. After all there is no such thing as 'normal'. That's because you are YOU and what you feel is individual to you and your mind and body. Having said that there are common elements to growing up. So let's get started with number one.

Chapter 1: It's normal to feel confused, to have doubts and worries and to feel nervous at times

If you ever feel doubtful about yourself or worried about growing up, you can be sure these feelings are very common and you're not alone. Why is growing up so confusing at times? Your grown-ups probably spent a lot of time teaching you the practical stuff like brushing your teeth, washing your hands before dinner, when to say 'please' and 'thank you' and tying shoe laces. However, when it came teaching you about what might be going on inside your head, you feel like you missed those classes, right? You're not alone.

Being a child can be confusing at times and it can be hard to work out why you're feeling worried or mixed up. If this happens to you then don't fear any more. It's totally fine. It simply shows that your mind is awakening to the possibilities of the world. You are realising the universe is awaiting you and the part you will play in it. And it is a rather big universe with so many opportunities that you start to feel not just a bit excited but maybe quite scared and daunted by it all.

The great news is that you don't have to take giant steps into the unknown. You should take things at a pace you are comfortable with. This will help you to stay in control, which in turn will help you to feel less nervous and less doubtful. Take plenty of time to make choices about your life. Don't let anybody hurry you into anything. You feeling doubtful and unsure is actually a really good sign - it shows that you are aware of the endless possibilities out in the world. You are intelligent and attentive. You are sensitive to what is going on and not just walking around numb.

The greatest doubters in the world end up asking all the right questions, for example, Newton, Edison, Hawking, Einstein, so be rest assured that you are in great company. Use it to your advantage and write lists of your questions. Maybe some of those questions you will not find direct answers to just now. There are some things we do feel unsure about and sometimes this can be our own internal warning system telling us to play it safe. Listening to your gut instinct is a good way of staying safe. There will be times in your life when you feel like taking a leap of faith and others when you don't feel it's right. Only you know what is right for you. Keeping a morning journal and filling it in every day before school can help you grow, and help you to control doubts. What's a morning journal? Every morning shortly after waking up you can use it to record:

- Three things you are good at

- Where you are going to focus your energies for that day. For example, you might really concentrate on being positive, or something as straight forward as smiling more, or aim to be on good terms with people you meet
- Three things to feel thankful for e.g. your health, your home, your family, your pet dog
- Goal(s) - split down into goals for that day e.g. making bed, being on time for school/lessons, eating three meals, have a pleasant conversation with one person
- Things to do that day - steps to achieving what you really want; so if you want to improve your long-term grades at school, this might start with getting your homework/assignments done by making a list of what needs doing and what equipment you need and in what order you'll do it with timeframes.

Keeping a morning journal can help you to focus your mind and free you of worry and doubt. This book has some lined pages at the back for you to use, if you don't have a journal, or you can use a notebook. You are awesome and you deserve to spend the time working out what your doubts are and how to manage them.

Remember, in life, doubts will come and go. But your awesomeness remains and you can achieve anything. Even very successful people like celebrities have doubts, probably more than most. It's often the case that people don't admit to having doubts because they think it shows weakness. When in fact people often gain a huge amount of respect for being honest about areas of doubt or insecurity. It shows we are all human after all.

"

I've questioned everything about myself, every step of the way. You have to have the same amount of fear and self-doubt as you do hope and blind optimism.

"

TAYLOR SWIFT

Chapter 2.1: Your 'normal' might be different to someone else's 'normal'

WHAT'S NORMAL ANY WAY?

There seems to be an obsession these days, more than ever, with humans to fit in with the 'norm', and what could be responsible is the fact that many of us use social media to splash our lives out there for all to see. This section discusses what's 'normal' (2.1) and also the (2.1) impact of social media on our perceptions of 'normal'. The truth is that 'normal' doesn't exist as a full scale, one-size-fits-all concept. Normal only exists for you and for people as individuals. In other words, everyone's 'normal' is different. Whatever is normal for you is what you feel is your M.O. or modus operandi.

What does that mean? Well, you've grown up with a particular set of family, friends, teachers, school experiences, values, behaviours, traditions, cultural influences, possibly religious or community influences. And you have taken all of that, consumed it, digested it, taken it on board, swirled it round and processed it in your consciousness for your entire life and now those experiences are central to your ideology about everything.

You are unique. That's not meant to be a compliment,

it's just a way of saying that there's only one you and you experience things through your own eyes.

MEET BLABBER-MOUTH

We've all been in a group of friends when someone with a very loud mouth has overheard something personal we have shared and then shouted across at us:

"EH? What on earth are you on about??? You did WHAT??? That's crazy! We never do that. We do this... We ALWAYS do it like this!" (...whatever it is they're on about).

If we were going to insert emoji here it would be the three monkeys covering their mouth, eyes and ears. How embarrassing. Not only have they embarrassed themselves, but you feel contradicted and put down. You may have shared a memory or an experience or an event coming up in your family or simply the way things are done at your house. And it is not the same experience as someone else who's listening. They can't help themselves but to blurt out that you're weird or strange and that you're some sort of outcast for not fitting in. After those random outbursts by so-called friends we feel ashamed and sometimes reluctant to speak about personal experiences again. But you need not worry, the person who shouts out at you is actually the one showing themselves up. They are the one who are showing that they have no manners, no thought for others and no understanding of the world. Their view of the world is limited to what they know. They feel uneasy about the fact that someone else might do something in a different way. In fact, they are exploiting the situation so that they are asserting their own experiences and views as 'normal' - all so that they can fit in and be accepted. Essentially trying to get themselves accepted by pushing out someone else. It's very much like behaviour of animals in a pack. There's always someone trying to be 'top-dog'. The best way to deal with it is to stay calm and don't feel ashamed. Remember that they are the one with the problem not you. Everyone else will be able to see that too - whether they show it on their faces or not.

It might be a good move to try to brush off situations like this with a simple 'yeah, yeah, whatever' and a wave of your hand. You'll find in time that both you and the group will actually feel pity for the shouting person, as they have shown themselves to be narrow-minded and limited in their knowledge and experiences. What's actually going on is that they haven't developed a sense of consideration of others yet - and some people never do unfortunately. It is a sign of immaturity and although they might be genuinely shocked at the different way you do things to them, difference among true friends should be handled with warmth, sensitivity, attempt at understanding and a listening ear. It may be that this person just isn't a true friend. In other words, no need to lose sleep over it.

Sometimes differences between friends can spark a meaningful, impromptu conversation or lively debate. As long as no one is being mean or rude and everyone is being respectful, you're in good company.

"

If you are always trying to be normal, you will never know how amazing you can be.

"

MAYA ANGELOU

Chapter 2.2: Following social media can damage your own special unique personality and your confidence

It is quite likely that your grown-ups sometimes worry about you being social media - and they have good reason to. Apart from the trolling and bullying that goes on, it can sometimes feel like people are bragging when posting too, and this is not healthy for anyone. These are the negative sides to social media.

Our personal development should be all about what is right for us and nurturing our own strengths and ambitions. What happens when we choose to scroll through social media posts can be the opposite of this. Viewing what's on social media can lead us to compare ourselves to others and what's out there. It can feel like people use social media to show off sometimes; and although this is not necessarily true it can leave us feeling a little jaded and upset. It can sometimes feel like people on social media are saying

- Look at me!
- Don't I lead an amazing life?

Some people have become passionate with posting their life story on social media. Even plates of dinner make it onto some people's posts. Why do you think they do that? It might be worth a debate if you're discussing this in a classroom setting.

Some people post things on social media just like a digital diary and their way to record their 'story' for themselves and their children. For some people it seems posting the 'right' kind of image is very important, so that they present themselves in the way they want to be perceived. It's our way of managing the public's understanding/perception of ourselves.

We all know that for social media posts can be a way to share lovely moments in our lives. It also can be a great way to share things with friends, like birthday and wedding photos; and it also can be a great way to stay in touch with friends who don't live nearby, like family who live abroad.

The facts is, whatever people's motivation to post, it can be unhelpful to get locked into comparing yourself and your life to the lives you see on social media. The reason for this is because your life is your own and isn't ever going to be the same as anyone else's. You have your own path.

Your 'normal' is what is understood by you, and your family, to be your common behaviour patterns, reactions and feelings. Everyone's family has their own way of living and doing things behind the doors of your family home. That's because no two families are the same and in fact no two people are the same. The bottom line is don't sweat social media. Enjoy it in small doses if you want to engage, but don't get sucked into it. You are enough without it; and all the follows, likes and comments in the world won't make you more popular, funnier, or better person, or help you to reach your goals. It can't replace actual human interaction where meaningful relationships are built and nurtured. Look up. Talk to people in person rather than just online.

Chapter 3: You are already ok

Sometimes we strive to be somebody else, when in fact you are already awesome just being you. You are in fact much more amazing than you realise. You are already ok. And you certainly don't need other people's approval, which can often be the driver for us to change ourselves.

It's normal for humans to want to improve their lives and themselves. And this is possibly somewhat responsible for driving us to want to change ourselves. When in fact we are already good just the way we are. This isn't just referring to physical appearance but can be applied to our personality.

To be ambitious is great and this section is not about discouraging ambition. It's about saying - yes go for your goals - but know that you're already a great individual with so much to offer and so much potential to achieve your goals.

Be confident in who you are and your ability, but also be safe in the knowledge that regardless of what happens in the future (whether you reach exam target grades, pass driving tests, become a world-famous footballer) you are already a remarkable individual with many awesome achievements.

So far you have probably already achieved a huge amount and you should acknowledge your successes. Your brain has probably already learned to do one of the hardest jobs it'll ever take on - learn to walk. Yes, this is true. Balance is extremely tricky for your brain to control. And looking at this list below how many of these things have you already achieved? Your body is an incredible machine and you're the one at the steering wheel:

- Learning to read and write
- Learning to ride a bike
- Learning the words to a song
- Learning to play a musical instrument
- Learning to speak a foreign language
- Learning to speak in the first place
- Trying out any challenging hobbies - e.g. dancing, playing a sport, sewing, drama, ice-skating, hockey, martial arts
- Being a good friend and learning social intelligence.

Every day you are already continuing to achieve so much and have ALREADY achieved so much. If you have an appetite to change something about yourself, think about **the reasons** for your desire to change. Is it because you want to be seen in a different way? Is it because you want to have a certain reputation among your peers or community?

Whatever the driver - remember you are already ok. Don't go doing something drastic with your physical appearance or personality just to please someone else. It will not make you happy in the long term.

"

It takes courage to grow up and become who you really are.

"

e.e. cummings

Chapter 4: When grown-ups get mad at you, it's usually not your fault

Grown-ups sometimes shout; well, many do at some point in their lives, let's face it. Grown-ups shout at each other on occasion and sometimes at children. This feels awful when it's happening when it's directed at you. It can leave you feeling upset, small, unsettled and even unsafe. What you should know, is that it's likely not you that's caused them to be so angry - unless of course you really have done something indefensible, like invite all of your friends over for an all-night party without their permission. That's not clever. Please don't try that.

There is a belief among many, that all behaviour is a message. We know that nobody is perfect and people's levels of patience are all different, and some people shout much quicker than others. Grown-ups who are shouting, are usually trying to communicate a message. They might be trying to say a number of things, such as:

- *You're not listening to me so I'm going to try saying it in the loudest possible version!* - This is probably the number one reason parents or teachers shout. The child hasn't responded to a request despite being asked several times. It drives grown-ups crazy! They might have asked you a few times already to do something and you haven't done it. In this case, the child sometimes (dare I say conveniently) doesn't hear the request, due to being engrossed in a game, book or other activity and therefore the grown-up gets angry, as it appears that they have been ignored. Nobody likes being ignored. Hence the shouting.

- *I'm in a situation - I don't know what to do and now I'm feeling helpless and out of my depth!* This might be the furthest thing from your mind but grown-ups don't have all the answers and they often wish they had a rule book for life that told them exactly what to do. It doesn't exist unfortunately. Panic can induce fear and that can result in shouting. Still can look and feel very scary though.

- *I'm realllllly stressed, I feel like I'm losing the plot and don't feel like I have any control over anything in my life!* - They may be stressed from something such as relationships, work, financial pressures - this can cause a lot of shouting.

- *I'm upset and anxious - help?!* - They may be feeling upset from a series of events - a chain of events that has left them feeling quite frankly helpless and anxious. It may be a request for help.

- Some parents are shouty* - maybe they picked it up from their parents, in which case try to break the chain if you can.

Try not to wind up being shouty with your family and friends. Make a promise to yourself that you'll not copy this behaviour.

*Important note:** one thing you should never tolerate from parents, family, friends or school staff is constant shouting, and this might be by those who seem to have uncontrollable anger issues. This is unacceptable and you should tell someone. Grown-ups who go on like that need help with their anger and they mustn't be allowed to treat you or anyone else on this way. Most families have an occasional showdown where there's a row or an argument but if you are subject to regular or even daily shouting and verbal abuse from someone at home or school, do not put up with this. Report it to a trusted grown-up and make sure you are heard and that you are clear on what is happening. Things can be done to help grown-ups with anger problems.

Alcohol sometimes makes grown-ups turn nasty and start shouting. Again, this is not something you should have to tolerate and it's never your fault. Parents and teachers should not be frightening to you either.

Shouting can cause more stress for the person shouting, so rather than helping them to feel better, like they're getting something off their chest, it can result in them feeling worse and can also make them feel rotten afterwards for how they have behaved. Most of the time it's best to let people cool off and give them a bit of space. But you should never apologise for their behaviour, or for them shouting at you. Grown-ups who are genuinely sorry for shouting and who had a momentary blip, will usually come and apologise once they've calmed down.

What to take away from this chapter is that the problem rests with the grown-up who is shouting, not the child. There are ways to engage children so that they carry out requests (e.g. helping with the chores, brushing their teeth, doing their homework etc) without shouting. Just some grown-ups are better at this than others and some have more experience and patience. There are parents who are just so laid back they never seem to shout. Some people are not as highly-strung as others. It all depends on the individual. Football managers are the same I expect. When grown-ups shout it gets them in a knot. Make sure it doesn't also get you in a knot otherwise it can affect your self-esteem and confidence.

Chapter 5: Not everyone can manage to eat 5-a-day

Eating a variety of fruits and vegetables is considered healthy for humans, by doctors and medical professionals. No doubt about it. Scientists have proved time after time the power of plant-based foods and the wonders they can do for the human body. And it is important that we stay healthy. Some foods are even called super-foods, like they have a superhero status. Blueberries are one fruit that in recent years has gained this status. The current government advice in the UK is to eat five fruit and/or vegetables per day. And in fact, that ten portions is 'better'. Getting your five-a-day can include eating something as simple an apple, eaten raw at snack time; carrot batons; cherries, an orange; and for others their five-a-day might include eating a spaghetti and sauce, containing onions, tomatoes, carrots and courgette for example. People choose to eat their healthy foods in a variety of different ways. Some prefer raw, some liked it cooked. Some a mixture of both.

When babies start out eating foods other than milk, at around 6 months old, the advice given to parents is to feed them healthy pureed fruits and vegetables, such as a well-blended homemade chicken and vegetable soup. No nasties and no added salt or sugar. We also know that a freshly prepared meal is better for us than a processed meal. And cooking things ourselves means we know what is in our food and that there are no added preservatives. Adding too much salt and sugar is also not good practice.

The current advice from the World Health Organisation (W.H.O.) is to eat five portions of fruit and veg per day - that's in total, not of each. A portion of fruit or vegetables is considered to be around 80g. And eating these the W.H.O. believes can lower the risk of serious health problems such as heart disease, cancer and stroke.

Apart from this fruit and veg are full of minerals and vitamins and a great source of fibre to keep your bowels moving. Fruit and veg are generally low in fat and can form part of a healthy balanced diet.

So this is all great .. and you've been taught this before, on more than one occasion. Nutritional advice about what's good and what's not, is even written on the side of cereal packets for us to digest with our breakfast each morning. And school have sent home umpteen-dozen letters about it over the past few years. 5-a-day, fruit and veg, eat your greens, sugar is bad, yadda, yadda, yadda.

What no one tells you is that everyone's tummy/bowels/intestines are different. Some people's tummies simply cannot cope with 5-a-day. Fruit and veg can give people gas or wind in their tummies, and sometimes bloating when their tummy is full of gas.

Take baked beans for example, a common enough food. Loads of people love beans on toast. These often cause people to turn into Mr or Mrs trumpet trousers. And it can be rather funny - let's be honest. For most people this isn't a problem. Just a bit of gas and a little snigger between friends or family members. But occasionally people really suffer rather bad ill-effects from eating gassy foods. And this can cause tummy pains or frequent trips to the toilet. As you grow up you will start to realise what foods are ok for you and which ones cause you discomfort - if any. Some people don't suffer any ill effects from any foods. Some people can't eat one or two individual things as they cause cramping or maybe a bit of diarrhoea. Generally young people need plenty of nutrition, plenty of fibre, plenty of water (keep hydrated) and plenty of sleep (at the right time of the night!). You're still growing after all and your brain is still developing. Putting good nutrition into your body will mean you have the best chances of being the best version of you. Shiny hair, sparkly eyes, feeling alert and focused, great skin, and above all a healthy you.

Listen to your body and talk to a GP, doctor or health care professional for expert advice on healthy eating. Diet-specialists, called dieticians, can help with planning healthy meal ideas if you would need specific advice tailored to you.

"

You are what you eat. So don't be fast, cheap, cheesy or fake.
"

ANONYMOUS

Chapter 6: Taking risks can be good if they're the right risks

I spoke to several groups of children about this chapter before writing it and asked them about their attitude to risk. What was apparent was that each person's attitude to risk was different and each child had their own reasons for feeling the way they did when describing a risk, they either would or would not take.

When asked to imagine a risky scenario, one child described someone diving off a cliff hoping to reach a body of water below. They said they themselves "absolutely - would not" be prepared to take a risk like this for any reward. They described the fact that there was no certainty they would make it to the water without injury or even causing their own death and therefore it made no sense to imagine that taking this risk was an option. For them that was beyond the limits of anything reasonable and most of us would agree. For most people this is good common sense, and this type of risk is one that most of us just wouldn't take. Human behaviour generally navigates the world with sensible calculated risk and this generally mitigates against harming oneself and causing injury or death to one's own body. And thank goodness for that otherwise we'd all be diving off dangerous cliffs senselessly and mindlessly hoping for the best. Not clever.

What about other risks? Well as one child put it, it really depends on the risk. You have to be able to afford to lose whatever you're risking and, in the case above, losing your life or incurring serious injury isn't an option. Taking a risk means putting on the line and offering up whatever you're risking and on the off-chance you don't succeed, losing everything you're risking. Grown-ups who become addicted to gambling often get stuck in a cycle of taking risks they can't financially afford and this can cause huge misery to themselves, their families and the friends. So risks can be dangerous in more than one way. There are lots of other considerations around risks. Let's take a look.

Safeguarding
A parent's job, as well instinct, is to protect and guard their children against harm and hurt. It is also one of the key roles of the school to safeguard children while in their care. While at school the school staff are what's known as 'in loco parentis' meaning 'in place of the parent'. Safeguarding is written into schools' and government policies and staff are trained on how to keep children in schools safe.

Parents, as well as teachers, as you have probably seen, are easily thrown into a panic and raise the alarm when it comes to the suggestion of children taking on uncalculated risks. This is to keep you from harm.

Examples of risk you might ask to take at home might include:

- *Can I walk home from ***'s house by myself?*
- *Can I play out for one more hour in the dark?*
- *Can I go to the shopping centre / mall with my friends?*
- *Can I go to the party at ***'s house?*

These are all terrifying situations for parents because the first thoughts they have are all about the risks and potential threats to the child. Most parents know that the child must grow up and in order to do this and to learn and experience life, some risks are necessary.

Check out a poem called 'Nettles' by one concerned parent, Vernon Scannell. It's about dreading the moment when he knew his three-year-old son would once again fall in the nettles behind the garden shed, a mistake he'd witnessed his son do once already and was excruciating to anticipate as a parent, even though he knew stepping back and letting go was the right move. It's available online and worth a read.

In this case Scannell knows he must let his son explore. He knows that his son will encounter the nettles and that they will sting and cause pain. But the nettles are not dangerous or life-threatening and he knows that his son must learn about the plants in the garden, even the nettles, albeit under his watchful eye. This is what is known as a controlled risk.

Parents often find it hard to watch their children taking risks but they also understand that taking controlled risks is a way of learning and part of growing up.

In fact, controlled risks are generally good for children and can benefit children growing up. It improves their understanding of the world.

Other examples of controlled risks might be:

- Trying something new, breaking away from a trusted routine or from something familiar and maybe trying out a new club or team; maybe you might try out learning a new skill; who knows you might love it you might not. But who is to know unless you try? It's a risk that you might not know anyone when you get there, but then again you might leave with some new friends.

- Having open discussions with friends or class-mates - telling them your opinions on matters and not just saying what you think they might want to hear, but also keeping in the expectation of politeness and respectfulness towards each other.

- Choosing something new and unfamiliar such as trying a new food, working with a new group of classmates on a school project, making a new friend at break time.

A healthy level of curiosity and undertaking some decision-making as a child, with the support and permission of your parents, is an important part of growing up.

Yes, some parents are more cautious than others and appear to be stricter. Some appear more laid back and this isn't always a good thing, even though you probably wish it was your parents who were less strict. Everything comes in good time.

So yes, some risks are good and they're generally good because you have talked them over with your grown-ups/parents or teachers first and talked over the possible outcomes, highlighted the possible pitfalls and worked out what is actually involved before you start.

Don't be shy talking to your parents about things you would like to do - they were your age once, and they remember what's it like to be curious. They are there to protect you and love you and they are aware of things that you aren't yet. They have experience and knowledge that is yet to come to you. You will grow up and become an adult and then be in charge of your own risks. Just remember to check things out first before diving into something headlong that you can't get out of.

"

The more risks you allow children to take, the better they learn to take care of themselves.

"

ROALD DAHL

Chapter 7: Some friendships are 'real' and some are 'fake'

A useful checklist

A good friend:
• is kind
• returns calls and messages
• is there / is present
• listens to you
• respects your feelings and opinions
• does not get angry when you refuse to do something
• does not make you do something against your will
• reciprocates and shares
• consults you when making decisions that matter to you both
• is honest
• behaves with integrity towards you and others - this means with courtesy, honour and respect
• is consistent - does not chop and change their minds every two minutes, confusing everyone around them

When you decide to invest in a friendship and taking a chance at becoming someone's friend, you can't always tell from the outset if they are going to invest in you in the same way in return. What is meant by 'real' friendships are genuine friendships, where people are consistently sincere and caring. These friendships, like any good relationships require work and commitment.

Friendships require much more than two people to value each other, to put in the effort and make the time for each other; genuine and lasting friendships can require putting someone else's feelings before your own at times. It comes as quite a shock to some people when they realise that meaningful friendships do require a good deal of effort and commitment. It's also about being thoughtful, caring about someone and looking out for them. But find a genuine friend and the rewards for you both are amazing. In a BBC poll these are the top five things people said they look for in a friend:

1. Trustworthiness
2. Understanding
3. Support
4. Sincerity
5. Loyalty

And let's be honest, none of these five things happen by accident or without effort. They require thoughtfulness, selflessness, knowing the difference between right and wrong and a moral compass. Let's take one at a time and unpick what each one means.

Trustworthiness
You may have seen or been part of one of those team bonding activity days, where a team of four or five people stand behind a friend or colleague and catch them while they fall back. A somewhat scary example of placing your safety entirely in someone else's hands. Quite a lot of fun, but the serious point to those trust exercises is a way of physically demonstrating the trust we sometimes place in others. We take a chance in trusting someone for example when we ask a friend to:

- Be there - be reliable - when we need them most
- Give us their honest and truthful opinion
- Look after something important to us
- Keep something private or secret
- Not to do something deliberately to upset us.

These examples of trust are linked with 'loyalty' which we'll come to later on. When trust is broken it can be devastating and very difficult to then place trust in that person again in future. Broken trust often results in broken friendships. The thought is planted in our minds that if this person has let us down once, then it's possible they might do it again. And let's not forget that it hurts to be let down; it can be a feeling that lasts a long time when someone breaks your trust. What's the answer? The answer is to invest in smart friendships -

these are ones where you don't take great big leaps of faith right at the start of meeting someone, or even a few days into a friendship. You take small steps for some time, enough time so that you feel sure that you've got a good friend before you take great big chances and place great trust in someone. All too often we hear stories on the news about people who have transferred all their money and their life savings over to a 'friend' in another part of the world, a friend who approached them, whom they met on the internet, on Facebook or Twitter or even a dating site. And then they never hear another word. Gone. Without trace. Private investigations reveal nothing and their bank can do nothing to retrieve their money as it was sent with their authority. They've essentially been tricked; lured into a false sense of trust by a fake friendship by someone being dishonest, deceitful and fraudulent. We wonder how this type of thing happens as it seems so obvious and so stupid to fall into this trap. However, some people are experts at luring us into being their friend and manipulating us into ultimately getting something from us that they want, whether it's money, status, or whatever. We need to have our wits about us when choosing friends. Smart friendships are all about taking it slowly and not giving anything valuable away too soon. Believe in your instincts regarding trust. If you feel unsure or hesitate to trust someone for some reason (even if you can't quite pin-point the problem) then you are probably right to be suspicious. Don't place your trust in someone you hardly know or in someone you're at all unsure about.

Understanding

This is about seeing things from someone else's point of view, sometimes called empathy. In truth we can never actually empathise with anyone else entirely. We are all unique individuals and different; therefore, we all have our unique individual thoughts, feelings, reactions and responses. When someone says 'I understand how you must be feeling' it is a poorly constructed expression which can never really be true. It would be better for us to ask of each other 'how are you feeling?' or 'I hope you're feeling ok' or 'I'm here if you want to talk' rather than assume we understand someone else's mind. But in friendship understanding is about getting to know someone's circumstances, their life, their way of doing things and spotting when we might be of help or comfort. Understanding cannot be acquired quickly. It takes time and a wide range of experiences together before two friends truly understand each other. Part of the fun of friendship can be going on this journey together, a journey of discovery.

Sometimes we meet someone in life and we just seem to 'click'. They seem to understand us and we seem to understand them. This type of genuine understanding is rare but not impossible. Understanding can be down to context. For example, someone might understand you in a school context, meaning that they get to know you in school, but they don't know what you're like outside of school, at home for example, or at Jiu Jitsu, swimming, football, and they might not know you have other parts to your life which bring out different sides to your personality. This can be why people have lots of different friendship groups and this can be good for several reasons. You might have your friends from school, different friends from your hobbies, family friends, and so on. And this could be the same when you grow into an adult. It's healthy to have different groups of friends so that you can open your mind to different experiences and cultures, different ways of doing things, and it means that if one group of friends has a fall out or disagreement, you're not left feeling isolated; you'll always have other friends to spend time with while things cool off with the fallen out group.

The bottom line with understanding is that we should try our best to understand each other and real friends spend time listening to each other to make sure they understand. Good understanding is brought about by good communication. How many arguments have you heard end with "you just don't understand!!!!" before the person then storms off? It's a common complaint from human beings that we don't understand each other. Sometimes trying to explain what we feel can be tricky too, so take your time.

A warning here that texting and messaging 'friends' isn't the best way of explain your feelings when things get heated. Talking is always the best means of communicating when friends are trying to understand each other. Texts can be misinterpreted, and nobody is ever really sure of the tone of a text message, which leaves them open to being misunderstood. The other thing about typing a message is that the message can be shown to others or forwarded on, causing acute embarrassment. It is hurtful and an open betrayal of trust when someone shows a message only intended for them to others. So don't type / write anything down and send it unless you would be happy for others to read it.

Support

The giving and receiving of support between friends can be described as emotional care and attention for each other. Good friends help to look after each other and boost each other's emotional well-being. It's not just about remembering birthdays and being on time when meeting up. It's about being there and offering to help when times are difficult; it's about being able to read situations and work out what might be the most helpful for your friend. Sometimes friends need space and to know that you're there if they need you. If you have friends like this who are sensitive to your needs and give you just the right level of support you need then these are good friends. Friends who are not genuine might not be there when you really need their support. Then there are people who like to be the centre of a crisis and will meddle in your affairs pretending to be supportive when they are actually just there for themselves. They might even be there to dig up some private information only to betray you by sharing with a third party. You definitely don't need people like this around.

How many friends should we have?

There is a belief that in life most of us have 3 or 4 real friends at the most and that everyone else we know are what we call acquaintances. Acquaintances are contacts, connections, people who you know and who you are familiar with, but that you don't share your private stuff with. It's ok to have lots of acquaintances.

You might receive a little support from them from time to time to. But only share your private matters with your genuine friends if it makes you comfortable to do so. If in doubt: keep close counsel. In other words, tell nobody anything. Keep your business private unless you trust the friend you're telling one hundred percent.

Sincerity

How many friends have ever done something for you without expecting something in return? This is a true sign of sincere friendship. There are occasions when a friend does something so nice for you and you don't even find out about it that day or the next, but maybe years down the line. This is friendship gold. They might have stepped aside and let you do something in place of them. They might have stood up for you against a group of bullies. They might have sent you an anonymous valentine when you were feeling down, or ordered your favourite milkshake and left it on your doorstep as a surprise. Sometimes you can identify exactly which friend it is by the treat or kindness. This level of care and consideration reveals a great deal about the friend who shows it.

Sincere friendships are also built when real friends come together regardless of their differences. Two friends might have different opinions and ideas; however, they can still learn from each other and grow through the friendship. You may have not seen in each in a long while, but the time spent apart hasn't lessened how you feel about your friendship.

There are tricky times for all friendships none more so than when a friend must deliver some home truths - with sensitivity and clarity. Maybe you have been unkind to your family and your friend takes time to point it out that you've lost your focus on what's important. Maybe you're hanging around with the 'wrong sort' and your true friend stops you to say exactly what they think about it all. You don't want to hear it but deep down you know they're right.

It takes a lot of guts to confront someone to save them from being hurt in the long run. They're willing to risk your friendship in order to save you. However real friends are not malicious in doing so. They are not cruel or hateful with their words. They are sincere and always on your side. Remembering that the real friend has kept your deepest, darkest secrets for all this time might help you to see that they're genuinely trying to help you out with a bit of honesty at a difficult time.

Loyalty

"Loyalty means sticking by someone when they are down, whether they're right or wrong, but telling them when they are wrong and helping them get it right."

When friends show loyalty towards each other this is like reinforcing the friendship with cast iron. Loyalty can come in all sorts of different scenarios. Loyal friends:

- **Behave impartially** - they are open-minded and unprejudiced. This means they are accepting of you, who you are, your background, your choices, your culture and your upbringing
- **Are honest** - they express how they really feel in a non-malicious way
- **Do not place conditions on the friendships** - Loyal friends don't say for example "you have to wear XX brand to be my friend" Also payback is not the sign of a real friendship. There should be no "you do this for me, and I'll do this for you"
- **Have boundaries** - when a good friend shows loyalty, they also consider safe boundaries for you and them. If, for example, they believe you might be putting yourself in harm's way, they are going to break confidence and tell someone,

usually a grown up. Loyalty must be helpful rather than hurtful.

- **Don't indulge in gossip or spread rumours**
- **Stand up for you, especially in front of others**
- **Won't let you down.** They stick to fulfilling their commitments. If they say they're going to go and see the new film with you they go with you, even if their dream date asks them five minutes after you did.

Ultimately, it's dependability and everything listed above rolled into one. You can depend upon your real friends, and if you can't, then they're not your real friends. Protecting each other and looking out for each other's well-being is what true loyalty and friendship is about.

Like the other qualities above, loyalty says a lot about the person delivering it. They are strong and not easily swayed. They will make up their own mind and will be solid and resilient. Loyalty is a great quality in a human being if you're being loyal to the right person/people.

And finally.

Real friendships are worth sticking at. If it hasn't happened already, there will come a point when you do meet and bond with the right people for you. You may have, in the end, one or two real true friends and that's fine. It's not the volume of friends that you have that counts, it's the quality of the friendship.

A word about social media..
You may have lots of 'friends' social media platforms. However, these are not always from 'real' friendships. **And by the way, you should stay away from making online connections with people you've never met.** Real friends know each other in person and have meaningful conversations face to face. Lots of people spend lots of time on social media 'engaging' and wonder why they are still lonely. The best thing to do is get out and do something real - join a club, go wall climbing, go to the movies with a friend. Look up from your phone and see the world. Make real connections with real people and ask them how they're doing. Extraordinary things happen real people come together.

"

You can't change how people treat you or what they say about you. All you can do is change how you react to it.

"

MAHATMA GANDHI

Chapter 8: It's ok if you don't know what you want to do when you leave school/college/university. Some people spend a lifetime trying to work this out

There's sometimes a lot of conversations held with young people about making choices, particularly choices about what you want to do when you leave school. It is after all a huge decision. It is a commitment which says "I want to do this or that job" when in fact you've never even tried it, not even for one day in most cases. Put like that, it's a crazy thing to ask anybody, but especially a teenager who has spent most of their life behind school doors. Work experience may or may not have been organised by your parents or your school. So you may not have had the chance to get out into the world of work. The chances are that if you have been into the workplace it has only been briefly, maybe for a week at the most and it was to try out one job, one role in one organisation. You deserve to be in a job that you love and I mean really love. One where you excel because you're using and developing your skills and talents. Nobody wants you to end up doing something you hate doing. You are worth so much more than that. You have spent so much time and effort getting to this point in your life that you can't let your future be shaped by chance. Let's get you on a journey, a thinking journey.

Admittedly there are a small group of people who do know what they want to do and who are sure 100% about it. When this happens to people it has usually been because of a life experience that has shaped their future. For example, Professor Stephen Westaby, the cardiac surgeon who fitted the UK's first artificial heart pump, knew from very early on that he wanted to be a pioneering heart surgeon. This is because when he was a youngster he witnessed his grandfather having a heart attack while out on a walk with the dog. It was that moment he said, that made up his mind about his career. You might call that a calling. If you're in this category then great. Your job now is to find out the steps to becoming your dream job. Talk to people in your dream job and ask them how they got there. Not many of us experience these epiphanies or moments of clarity. Most of us drift between ideas of jobs, humming and harring, unsure about which decisions to make, all the while feeling the pressure to decide. In the end all that matters is that you keep moving, preferably forwards, but keep moving nonetheless. What do we mean by this? Keep moving forward? It means just keep doing something positive with your time when you do leave school, like learning, working at a skill that is useful. Develop yourself in some way and don't sit about the house once you leave school playing computer games, getting on your family's nerves because you never open your curtains, comb your hair or shower. Keeping on moving means you don't have to make a final decision just yet about a career and have it bind you into a lock down situation for the rest of your life. It can be useful to make a list of all the things that interest you in life, even if you've never tried them before. Because whichever career you choose it definitely helps if it's something that you like to do.

Take for example wall climbing. You may have been doing this as a hobby for some time. Could it be something you get into as a career? The way to explore that would be to talk to the people in charge at the local centre and ask how they got into being climbing coaches. Making connections with people, talking to them, known as 'networking', is generally a really good way of establishing good contacts and finding out information. You'll not find all the answers you need on Google sitting in your bedroom. We know that's one way but it's not the way to fully expand your horizons. You are worth so much more than that and everyone wants you to do well, your parents, your family, your friends and your teachers. Invest some time in yourself. You are amazing and we want to make sure you stay that way. All the work you have done so far to get to this stage, all the difficult times you have endured, you are truly awesome, and you should never stop realising that.

Make a list of the things you are good at and the things you are interested in.

Here's an example:

Good at / interested in	Not so good at / not interested in
Love working outdoors	Working indoors
Visiting new places	Computers / sitting at a desk
Wearing a uniform	Being my own boss
Don't mind getting my hands dirty	Working by myself
Team work but with some parts where I am responsible for things myself	Working in schools/education

Now your turn. Fill in this table and take time to really think about what you like to do.

Good at / interested in	Not so good at / not interested in

Now write down

- One or two grown-ups who will help you / mentor you on your quest to find the right job? Might be a family member or teacher that you feel happy talking to. Write down their names.

_____

_____

_____

- Any grown-ups already in your dream job, whether you know them or not? You might be able to talk to them directly or write / email them if you got an address.

_____

_____

_____

- A few jobs you might be interested in that you will find out more about

_____

_____

_____

You are worth it - so spending time thinking over your future. Use the lined pages at the back of this book or use a notepad and grab a pen. Start making lists, make notes, scribble down ideas, write down the names of people you admire and ask yourself what is it about them that you like? Talk to people from a range of different jobs and ask them what their experiences are like on a day to day basis. They will probably be very honest with you about their experiences. Whatever you do don't bury yourself away in your bedroom. No one ever got their dream job by doing that. You can be anything you want to be. There are no limitations - only your imagination can set the boundaries for that. Be your own champion and go be you, whoever you want to be! It's all out there for you. Be who you want to be - just don't forget to be yourself.

Chapter 9: Sometimes grown-ups get it wrong

Believe it or not this is true. You will have seen it happen lots of times. Has your grown-up ever:

- Forgot your lunch money on the first day back at school or sent you into school on a staff training day?
- Made a snap decision in the heat of the moment? - *"Right that's it - no iPad for a whole year!!! No TV ever again. No biscuits. No friends ever again!!! Oh and you're grounded FOR LIFE!!!!"* Sound familiar?
- Missed and event / forgot to take you somewhere? e.g. to your friend's birthday party
- Totally over-reacted to something? e.g. throwing towels and toothbrushes around the bathroom like a crazy person when you say you've brushed your teeth and you haven't
- Punished everyone in the house when something goes wrong? Like screaming at the top of their voice for a full five minutes before cancelling a family trip to the beach because your little sister has smeared thick swathes of expensive hand cream all over the freshly painted living room walls.

You get the idea. You might possibly have your own stories to tell. We all do in fact. It's part of life and growing up.

However instead of cooling off, calming down, taking a deep breath and admitting our mistakes, grown-ups become good at smoothing over or hiding their mistakes and failures, overreactions and wrong decisions, and sometimes dress them up as intentional... "oh yeah, I meant to leave booking your birthday party until last minute just so we could see who you wanted to invite nearer the time," really means... *"I've been so busy with work, managing and looking after the family / our home that I haven't got around to doing that yet. Sorry ... Life is so damn busy. I love you and I just need a HOLIDAY!!!"*

It would be far more effective and honest if grown-ups shared their mistakes with their children. "Hey, I got that wrong.. sorry." This would help children to realise that mistakes are part of life and normal. We are not robots and therefore mistakes are inevitable. Normalising them would be helpful for everybody. Instead we make out as though everything we do is intentional and perfect and consequently set up our own children for disappointment when they cannot be 'perfect' too. The reality is that everyone gets it wrong sometimes - without exception - everyone.

As you grow from childhood into adulthood, nobody really quite tells you how to become a successful grown-up. As you grow up, lots of people spend lots of time telling you what not to do, like at school and at home. That leaves a huge gaping hole of possibility as to what is exactly required to be an effective grown-up. It's like we're meant to work out for ourselves what is all the right stuff going on around us, absorb it and become it, and ignore all the bad stuff. Essentially a giant guessing game of sorts: of learning by example - watching others - picking up what to do / what not to do by observing what's happening around us. Tricky, requires guidance, patience and trial and error.

The same can be said for becoming a parent. THE most incredible, THE most astonishing thing is that nobody teaches you how to parent and yet it is an enormously important and challenging role, lasting years and years. When you arrive home with your new family there are all sorts of skills to learn, including the practical stuff like looking after your child's physical well-being - nappies, feeding, hygiene, toilet training, safety around the home, brushing teeth, looking after them when they're poorly. Every new situation is a huge learning curve and as these often occur spontaneously they leave some of us reeling. Adults have the following in varying amounts and combinations, so it's a bit of a lottery as to knowing how an adult will manage with being a grown-up or a parent:

- intuition / instincts
- intelligence
- common sense
- experience

Truth is, apart from these, we're mainly guessing. Shocking. Don't tell anybody.

Grown-ups respond to parenting in different ways. Some people make really good parents and seem to be so natural in acquiring of parenting skills. They are generally calm and have a relaxed appearance when around children and seem to know naturally what is the best options are in each situation. Most of all they give themselves time to think before they act. Other parents struggle to cope with the enormity of the job of parenting, plus the responsibility that goes with it and try to muddle through best they can. Most people fall somewhere in the middle, and do an ok job most of the time.

It all depends on the adult, their personality, their understanding of good parenting and their view of the world (including how they were brought up). Whatever type of parenting you receive, your job is to keep yourself growing, not to change others. However one thing is guaranteed, all parents make mistakes, even the super cool, super chilled ones. And as you grow up you too will find that you make mistakes, however don't beat yourself up about it. Sometimes making a mistake can lead to a positive outcome:

- it can teach us important lessons about life
- it reminds us we're not perfect and that we're human not robots/machines
- it means we can try again
- it makes us grow as a person - we learn more about the world around us
- it can fuel us to make the right choice/decision the next time - once you make a mistake you are determined to do better.

Most of all one mistake does not dictate the rest of your life. Forgetting your lunch money doesn't mean that your grown-up doesn't love you, just that they've got a lot on their minds. Wouldn't it be great if once in a while we could all give each other a hug and say "it's ok, remember we're only human".

Chapter 10.1: Everybody's got to wash the kitchen floor sometimes

What does the title of this chapter refer to? Washing the kitchen floor? This metaphor is saying that sometimes things or jobs that need to be done are not glamorous, desirable or exciting, but they just need doing, for life to continue in a happy and healthy way. Life is full of 'jobs' and chores like washing the kitchen floor. Here are a few that might be similar for you:

- Doing homework
- Brushing your teeth; washing your face; brushing your hair
- Staying in to revise for an exam
- Setting the dinner table
- Doing the dishes after a meal
- Making your bed
- Tidying your bedroom
- Helping out with chores at home

All these things are part of life and probably a regular part your world and keep everything ticking round. Especially important is the one about brushing your teeth and washing. These are daily essentials to everyone's routine. To be accepted in society we must present ourselves in a way which is not offensive or even remotely disgusting and keeping on top of our personal hygiene is one way of making sure we don't smell or have yellowing teeth. But who likes to climb out of a nice warm bed and step into a shower in the morning? Probably not everyone. It's just one of those jobs we must do to make sure we look after ourselves. These types of jobs, like washing the kitchen floor, are best scheduled for certain times in the week, put them on repeat for the same times next week and just do them, get them done and don't moan about them. They are not the most exciting or the most interesting things to be doing but they are nonetheless important in their own ways. Don't overthink jobs like these. Sitting around and moaning about what needs to be done is a way of dragging your mood down and the mood of everyone around you. Don't waste time moaning. Get up and crack on with living your life, and following your own path.

Making your bed in the morning before you leave the house, some psychologists believe, is key to having a great day. Some believe that if you set the tone for your day right from the start, it will have an impact on the rest of your day. So starting in a positive way might involve

- getting up on time
- having a wash
- making your bed
- getting breakfast and tidying away your dishes

and this might be the focused and orderly way to set the positive vibe for the rest of your day. If you're rushed in the mornings getting out of the door, try setting your alarm for just ten minutes earlier and get up the first time it goes off. Don't press the snooze button. Doing that just puts you under unnecessary pressure. Don't make your day start that way.

Tip: check out Mel Robbins' 5 second rule - doing something positive within five seconds (such as getting up within five seconds of your alarm going off) is proven to have a positive impact on not only your day, but your mindset and success rates going forward.

If we're totally honest, deep down we would all love to ignore from time to time the nitty-gritty jobs like washing the kitchen floor but it's just not possible. If life was end-to-end excitement, splendid parties and stylish, trendy and dazzling outfits, in a short amount of time you would soon come to find all of that dull and boring. After all the reason a party is so exciting is because it's a break from our normal routine. It's safe to say that if you partied every day, you'd soon get bored of it. We all know the song that goes 'I wish it could be Christmas every day'. Well imagine if it really was Christmas every day.. the truth is that we would all become very bored of Christmas. Sounds unlikely but true. It's the fact that it only comes once a year that makes it special, like a birthday.

Life has its ups and downs, and is full of highs and lows. This is normal.

And here's an interesting fact: from the very start, doing chores around the house will help you to feel like part of the family. Sharing the tasks between people in a household is not only a fair way of doing things but it also means that you're working as a team. Chores shouldn't just be left to one person in a household. So if you know someone in your house who is always being left to do all the clearing up, washing, cleaning etc why not speak to them and work out just one job to start with that you could do every week, to lighten their load. It might be folding the laundry or feeding the family pet. But doing that regular job will make a big difference to them and also to how you feel in your family. It will ensure you feel like you have an important role in your family and you do.

Nobody said life would be fair all the time. Ranting "It's not fair!" is pointless. Life can be tough at times. It isn't all plain sailing. See 10.2 for an explanation of what 'plain sailing means'.

Chapter 10.2: Grown-ups sometimes speak using metaphor - and it can be so confusing!

There are lots of examples of metaphor in our language and people use metaphor sometimes to describe a situation that they might find otherwise difficult to put into words otherwise. Metaphor is a figure of speech. (Don't you just hate it when people give that definition?!) They dig people out of a hole - there I just used one - sorry! They dig people out of a hole when they can't think a way of describing something. This can be confusing as their meaning isn't always clear; but we can start by looking at an example, like when people say 'life isn't always plain sailing' - they're comparing life and the journey we have through life, to a smooth boat trip (plain sailing), saying that life isn't always like that. So a metaphor can be confusing the first time you hear it but once you know what it means it can actually be quite useful. Can you think of any more examples? Here are a few:

- The snow outside is a beautiful white carpet across the landscape
- She gave me an icy stare
- I had to pull out all the stops to win that football match

Also in our conversations we hear lots of idiomatic expressions. These are a type of informal language used in every day speech and often at first, they appear to make no sense at all. Here are some examples you've probably heard before:

- It's a piece of cake
- Kill two birds with one stone
- A bird in the hand is worth two in the bush
- It's raining cats and dogs

Another one - 'hummed and hawed' - this just means taking a long time to decide something and possibly refers to the actions you might do when trying to decide something - you might make those noises - humming and hawing - when thinking about how best to do something.

So as you grow up don't be surprised if you find yourself confused by metaphor and these other expressions. People learning English often say that these are very puzzling and can take a while to get the hang of. Sometimes people mix up metaphorical expressions - but that is a whole other book!

Chapter 11: Sometimes 5 and 6 out of 10 is ok

Sometimes 5 or 6 out of 10 is still ok. You don't always have to be 9/10 or 10/10. This isn't referring to scores in tests but more about the amount of stress you put on yourself to be perfect in every aspect of your life. Striving for perfection can actually be crippling and hinder progress, creativity and productivity. Working yourself into the ground is not healthy and is not going to end well in the long-term. Everyone needs to keep perspective on their own life and their work-life balance. The advice is to work moderately and take regular breaks. There are pinch points in most people's lives and times when things get hectic. That's normal. But don't live your life at one hundred miles an hour every day.

There is sometimes a vibe or message sent out to people not to give up until you've reached your target grades. "Don't stop until you reach perfection!" These can be inspiring statements but what they really mean is 'try your best'. That's all anyone ever expects of you. And this is what some people end up going around thinking, that they must try their best 100% of the time.

From being quite small you'll hear this phrase 'try your best' a lot. And it sounds fairly safe. It doesn't sound particularly dangerous, tiring or unmanageable.

However, it comes with a substantial health warning: **No one can try their best all the time.** This can be crippling and can lead to what is called 'burn-out' or exhaustion. Grown-ups and children who try their best all the time all end up suffering from this. What does it mean exactly?

It refers to negative results on your brain and body from the strain and stress that you place on yourself trying to be excellent all the time. Suffering from burn-out can have many symptoms, such as:

- Becoming grumpy, stop having fun, stop laughing at jokes
- Feeling like a failure
- Taking your frustration out on others
- Becoming judgemental and critical of others at school, work, because they don't live up to your standards
- Concentration becomes difficult
- You might over-sleep or conversely have trouble sleeping
- You might over-eat, or the opposite - lose your appetite at times
- You might feel that it's difficult for you to take time out, to relax and chill-out
- You might avoid the company of others at social gatherings and wish you were back home by yourself

- You might seek isolation more and more, and want to be on your own a lot of the time
- You might feel tired, helpless and lack motivation
- You might start experiencing headaches or nausea (feeling sick) or sore stomach or all of these
- You might lack enthusiasm for things in your life that you used to enjoy.

All these things can make you feel sad. And burn-out can cause this because your brain and body are trying to send you a message. They are trying to tell you to stop! The relentless speed of 'try your best' when applied all the time is too much for anyone, no matter the IQ or ambition.

If you experience any of these symptoms, tell your grown-up and ask to see the doctor or GP at your local doctor's surgery.

Here are some tips to help avoid burn-out.

Imagine your life as a bucket - well, don't over-fill that bucket, because if you do your body will kick back at some point and let you know. Our physical well-being always suffers when we don't get our work-life balance right. We become run down and can often fall sick.

Here are some examples of things you can do to make sure you don't overwork yourself:

- Don't join too many before/after-school clubs; only take on what is sensible
- Don't take on too many hobbies
- Don't take on too many friendships - a few friends are enough for anybody, you don't need loads
- Plan your week and your days so you have some time every day to relax - think about what you find relaxing e.g. going for a walk, watching TV, reading, meditating, listening to relaxing music, practicing yoga, taking a bath, getting outside in nature.
- Do make time for yourself - have some alone time - everyone needs alone time to give themselves room for self-reflection and self-development. This is time by themselves, maybe in your bedroom or a quiet room in the house. If you can't find a quiet room in your house you could go to a local bookstore, library or museum and spend half an hour there. These are generally quiet places to be.

Boredom

Here's a healthy fact: Being bored sometimes is ok. It is in fact good for us and can be good for your mental health. It can allow the mind to wander and 'daydreaming' can be great respite from the frantic lives we lead. Being bored does not mean that you're getting fed up of the game you're playing on the computer, or getting fed up of the videos you're watching over and over again. Be bold enough to step away from screens, work and other stress triggers long enough to let boredom set in. Let boredom set in the 'right' way. Go for a walk, swim up and down a local swimming pool, or just sit still with your eyes closed for 5 or 10 minutes. Let your mind empty of some of those things in your bucket. Let space drift through your thoughts. When you seek mental freedom and space and decide to go for a walk or swim, don't play any music during these times. Don't look for that type of stimulation.

Above all live moderately. Enjoy a range of things in moderation - have a little bit of each of these: hard work, fun, alone time, together time. Don't put a strain on your brain or your body. Respect both.

Chapter 12: Look after your mental well-being. Don't forget it as important as your physical - if not more important

Sometimes in life, you just need a hug.
No words, no advice, just a hug to make you feel better.

Looking after your thoughts and feelings is important and generally we refer to this as looking after our mental health or mental well-being, which refers to anything going on inside our heads/minds/brains. Physical well-being is all about the health of our actual bodies, the flesh and bones so to speak. Our physical well-being depends a lot upon our mental well-being. They are inter-linked.

What does that mean? Well, for starters it means that if you're feeling anxious, nervous, down or sad for a time, it can start to have a negative impact on your body and your overall health; for example, you might start getting a cold or feel flu-like symptoms, or maybe feel a tummy ache, or headaches or start to feel not quite right somehow or just not yourself. This 'not-right' feeling is sometimes called 'malaise'. Feeling run down can of course happen if we don't get enough nutrients and vitamins from our food as well. (Section five is where you will find discussion about healthy eating.) But this section is particularly about mental health and well-being, because your health is more than just about what you eat; it's about what you think, what you feel, what you say and what you believe. Before we go any further, if you have any concerns in this area, these are all matters that you can talk to your local doctor or nurse about at your local GP surgery. Don't be afraid to make an appointment to talk about a professional about mental or physical health. They are they to help everyone, not just grown-ups. There's always the option to talk to a trusted grown-up too. Sometimes talking about your feelings can help to make things feel better all round. You'd be surprised to know that many people feel down, anxious and depressed at some point in their lives and that talking can be a great therapy if you can find the right person to listen.

The thoughts and feelings we have can overwhelm us sometimes and can have profound physical effects on our bodies. One example might be someone having a panic attack. This could be described as when someone feels a sudden rush of intense anxiety and feels so overwhelmed by a situation or set of thoughts that their body can have a physical response such a fainting or a rush of blood to the head. Other physical symptoms of a panic attack can also include shaking, sweating, irregular heartbeats, feeling sick, feeling disorientated, dry mouth, restlessness and dizziness. At the moment when they occur, panic attacks, although the symptoms are not dangerous, can feel very frightening indeed for the person they're happening to. And for the days and sometimes months that follow after, can leave them feeling low in confidence and not wanting to go out or mix with others. Sometimes when faced with tough times people resort to unhelpful behaviours such as:

- Overeating - eating too much, and comfort eating
- Undereating - not eating enough, maybe due to loss of appetite
- Withdrawing - not going out, staying away from people
- Sleeping a lot
- Not sleeping enough
- Being aggressive and tempers flaring up easily
- Getting easily upset
- Using alcohol and drugs, thinking that they'll help them to 'escape' their problems.

None of these actually solve problems, but all in fact make matters worse. Short term they may appear to offer relief and respite from the world of problems buzzing round in our heads but none of them actually help to alleviate the problems. These behaviours create a vicious cycle, and only result in digging ourselves deeper into more problems. At the beginning of our problems for example, we may have anxiety and depression, and by the end we may have anxiety, depression and alcohol dependency.

Alcohol and mental health

Alcohol brings with it many problems of its own. It can affect the normal development of vital organs and functions, including the brain, liver, bones and hormones; and in addition, it can dehydrate us, makes us feel tired and can give us headaches and hangovers. Under the influence of alcohol, we can make bad decisions as alcohol can take away our ability to have clear judgement. On top of any mental health issues, no one wants to suffer these additional problems. Finding a solution to mental health issues, or finding a helpful and healthy strategy to help us cope with problems, is definitely the way forward, while the unhelpful behaviours listed above are taking a step backwards.

Get out into nature!

Start making healthy choices, not just healthy choices for your body but also for your mind. One way is to get out into nature. Go for a walk in a local park and find a seat where you can sit and enjoy looking at the trees and birds. Other ideas include: visit a local wildlife centre or aquarium, feed the ducks, go for a stroll in a local country park, spend time with a pet. There are many ideas for connecting to nature that are either free or low cost and that will have a really positive impact on your mental health. Do these regularly and prioritise them as important and quickly you will see how incredible the power of nature is. Our thoughts can at times dominate us and torment us but out in nature we can find mental freedom from the hectic and busy lives we lead; and an hour or two to breathe freely, stop thinking and over-thinking everything and just inhale fresh air.

Breathe!
Breathing is the most powerful and most natural thing we do and taking a moment to breathe can be a real boost to our physical and mental well-being. When we are in a panic or feeling anxious we breathe shorter, faster shallower breaths and it sends a signal to our brains that we need to be on alert. But there are ways to reverse this panic signal. If you're feeling anxious, try sending the signal to your brain that you're ok and there's no panic necessary. Do this by breathing deep, long slow breaths, spend a minute doing this every day, twice a day if you can and see the difference in your mood and overall outlook.

Recommended reading – *The Art of Breathing* by Danny Penman.

Extra Stuff

This section of the book contains activities that you may find useful at different times of your life. You can pick and choose which activity suits you at whatever time you feel is right. You don't have to complete these in the order that they appear here. Browse through them and get an idea of what's what. Then you can come back to them when you feel the time is right.

Activity 1. Visualisation task

There are some really useful tasks that can help you on your journey through life. One of them is called visualisation. Many people who use this every day find it helps them to focus on getting through a difficult event that's coming up or even to help them to achieve their goals in life.

It really does help, costs nothing and only takes a few minutes a day. A simple example of this is when my daughter used visualisation when she was first learning to ice skate. She found learning to stay upright on the ice just impossible as well as frustrating, and was worried about going to a friend's birthday party at the ice rink in case she couldn't stop falling over. It was not only painful falling over but so frustrating as she really tried and tried, even listening so carefully to the skating teacher's advice about how to skate. Before she went to sleep the night before the party, she spent a few minutes lying down with her eyes closed and imagined herself gliding gracefully on the ice and never falling over.

The results the next day were incredible. And this was after only one go at visualisation of ten minutes. By visualising herself being a successful skater, it was training her brain to believe she could skate and this had a positive effect when she actually tried skating the next day. This technique can be done for all sorts of things and is most effective when you use visualisation a few minutes a day. Whatever the skill or goal you are trying to achieve, imagine yourself doing that and being really good at it.

It only takes ten minutes of visualisation every day to train your mind into seeing and believing that the success is possible. Of course, you can't be guaranteed to pass your exams this way without doing the revision too, but if you are doing the revision and still feeling nervous about exams, then visualisation can help you to boost your confidence. Visualise yourself walking into the exam room, feeling up-beat, buoyant and positive, then sitting the exam and not feeling nervous but feeling strong and confident about completing your answers; and then imagine yourself at the end of the exam leaving the exam room with an assured and calm mood about you.

Activity 2. Letter to yourself task - self review

This letter writing activity is useful when you want to make changes in your life to improve things for yourself. It helps you to look back, then plan, then look forward. There is not a lot of point in regretting things that might have happened in the past. We can however, learn from what we have done, and these lessons are how we improve ourselves so we can live our best life.

1. Write down individual events and things that happened last year in your life, list them in the table
2. Then think of words to describe how each event made you feel. (See example below.)
3. In the 3rd column say how you could change things for the better the next time this happens.

Event	Word or words to describe how you felt	How could you change and improve things next time?
e.g. Didn't pass mock exam	Disappointed. Lost. Confused as I didn't really know how or what to revise.	Ask for specific revision advice at school; stick to a revision timetable; do some practice papers beforehand

This task will help you to identify what exactly went on for you previously, and enable you to dig down to see how you reacted to what is going on around you. Are all of your reactions negative? Positive? A mixture?

- Does this table, once completed, tell you anything that you can learn about yourself?
- Does it tell you how you might change things in future?
- What lessons can you learn from your past self?

Writing the letter

Write a letter to your future self, based on the table above, and once you've listed everything from your table, write some advice for your future self. <u>Underline the key bits of advice.</u> It might go something like this...

Letter example

Dear Fiona

Well last year was a good and bad year for you. A real mixture. It felt like a crazy year because most of the time I felt annoyed and angry at everyone. I feel moody sometimes and can't seem to get myself out of it. There were some good things however and they were:

- You started being friends with Isabella who turns out to be a really great mate
- You did really well in English and the teacher says you are on course for a good grade if you keep working the way you are
- You had nearly 100% attendance at school and you like most of your subjects
- You also got yourself organised and you were never late for school. You did this by getting yourself up on time in the mornings, which also meant you had time for breakfast and time to organise your school stuff

- You were allowed to go out with friends on an evening as long as Mum knew where you were
- You got a new mobile phone which was the one you wanted.

The main reasons for it being bad were:

- You didn't revise for your mathematics exam and this meant you didn't know how to answer lots of the questions; you only got 37%
- Your Mum got remarried and you don't like your Mum's new husband
- You lost your temper quite a few times with your Mum and had a lot arguments which got a bit shouty; this made you both feel rotten for ages afterwards
- You didn't always think of others - like when you went out to the cinema and didn't tell anyone where you were going. Mum was worried sick.
- You forgot your Mum's birthday
- You didn't go to visit your Grandma much and she misses you.

Although last year felt like a bad year there were actually some really great points. Life probably isn't as bad as you sometimes make out. There are many things to be thankful for and sometimes you just don't see it. Let's plan how to improve things. Here's some ideas that might be useful:

- Ask for help with revision - talk to a teacher that you get on with and ask what to do; are there any revision classes you could attend? Make sure you get a copy of the exam timetable and keep it where you can see it.
- Try to get along with those around you - you don't have to be best friends, just be polite and don't look for problems; remember that your Mum deserves happiness too.
- Try to keep calm when you're not happy about something; it doesn't help when you lose your temper. If someone tells you some news that you weren't expecting, try to stay cool and relaxed - give yourself time to thing over what the news really means - sometimes things aren't as bad as they first appear.
- Get organised with a list - make a list of jobs/events for yourself each week of things coming up that you need to do, like homework, going out with friends, birthdays coming up
- Ask your Mum for a list of family birthdays for the whole year - so you can buy a card or simply wish people a happy birthday on their special day. Pin this up where you can see it
- Make a promise to yourself to visit your Grandma and decide how regularly you think this might be possible (once a week/fortnight? Once a month?) stick to it. If you can't visit her

maybe send a card or give her a call to let you know you're thinking about her.

The fact that you've sat down to write this letter is a really good start. You can achieve anything you set your mind to. You are amazing and you are enough. Growing-up doesn't last forever. Enjoy each happy moment that comes along and remember that before too long you'll be the grown up who is confident, organised and calm, all because you took the time to set out a plan. Behaviour is your choice and we can all find happiness, relaxation and joy if we go about things the right way. Be strong and you can get through anything.

Yours truly,

Fiona

Activity 3. Goal Setting

Write down as many words as you can to describe **how you would like** this year ahead to be for you and how you would like things to turn out for you during the following year.

Here are some examples; feel free to come up with lots of your own.

- valued as a member of my family
- have happy friendships
- successful at a hobby/sport
- happy at home
- healthy, active
- academically and / or financially rewarding
- have fun-filled holidays.

Now picture yourself being successful in one of these scenarios. What is happening in that scene in your mind? Take a few minutes to 'see' the story in your mind. Don't have to write anything for this, just imagine it.

Here's an example: successful at school = collecting great exams results and teachers + parents being really happy for me. Everyone at school gathers round to lift me high in the air to celebrate my success. They are all smiling and giving me three cheers. I have a big smile on my face and I can't stop laughing. My adrenaline is running so fast through my body and I am feeling so amazing. I have got the exams results I wanted.

Now use visualisation technique described at the start of this chapter to close your eyes and visualise what that looks like in your own mind for a moment. Write down the steps you need to take to reach that goal. Below is an example written by a student, showing steps they would take to become more successful at school.

STEPS TO BECOMING MORE SUCCESSFUL AT SCHOOL:

1. Look over teachers' comments to see what advice they have given me to make improvements.
2. Finish all unfinished work.
3. Complete all classwork and homework to the best of my ability.
4. Read the feedback from teachers and act upon it.
5. Pay less attention to what others are doing and achieving and concentrate on my own path.
6. Spend less time on social media and playing on computer/phone/ technology. Build these in as treats when I deserve a break and that doesn't mean after 10 minutes. Put my phone down. Put it on silent or turn it off during periods of work.
7. Find out how to revise for exams and mock tests. Then revise.

8. Make a timetable. Make it realistic. For each day write down how much time I am going to spend working, and time built-in for relaxing. I'm going to make sure it's about 80% work, 20% relaxation (- and not the other way around!).
9. Don't leave homework until the last minute. Don't rush it and do a botch job when I know it's not going to get me the results I want.
10. Spend 1 minute each day with my eyes closed, visualising myself getting great results from school. With my eyes closed, I am going to imagine the way I feel when I achieve good results at school. It feels great.

Quite often you can find yourself already halfway to achieving your goals once you know which steps you need to take to get there. It opens the doors in your mind to achieving your goals. You already know 'why' you want to be successful at your goals. These steps are the HOW to get there.

What next?

Congratulations. You have reached the end... for now! If you have found this book useful it will be worthwhile keeping it nearby, as sometimes it can be handy to look at books again in the future. You can dip in and out of this book whenever you feel you need to. There are no limits on how many times you read a book.

I would love to hear how this book has been useful for you. Sometimes just one idea or sentence can really be helpful to you at a particular time in your life. And when you're fully grown up, it's still ok to refer back to this book if it helps to make things in your life clearer and more manageable.

You might recommend this book to a friend, or even a grown-up in your life who you think might find it helpful to spend a bit of time to think things over.

Read these positive affirmations to yourself at least once a day:

1. I am an amazing person

2. I will not compare myself to others

3. I learn from my mistakes

4. I am smart and capable of doing anything I put my mind to

5. Today I choose to be happy and to have positive thoughts

Above all remember - you are intelligent. You have begun an amazing journey into growing up. Among the joy and the happiness, there will be uncertainty. There will be times that are tricky and even difficult. It is how we deal with these times that defines us and shapes our view of the world. Stay positive and don't be afraid to ask for help when you need it.

(metaphor alert! -)

No person is an island.

You can use these lined pages to make notes, record ideas, write questions, write a morning journal or anything else you find helpful.

_____

_____

_____

_____

_____

Printed in Great Britain
by Amazon